COLLECTING
COCOONS

LOIS J. HUSSEY
and
CATHERINE PESSINO

COLLECTING

COCOONS

ILLUSTRATED BY
ISABEL SHERWIN HARRIS

THOMAS Y. CROWELL COMPANY NEW YORK

ACKNOWLEDGMENT   We are deeply grateful to Farida A. Wiley, Assistant Chairman, Department of Public Instruction, The American Museum of Natural History, who has always helped and encouraged us in our study of natural history. We wish to thank the staff of the Peabody Museum, Yale University, for their invaluable aid in furnishing specimens and other material for illustration, and the New York State College of Agriculture, Cornell University, for permission to use the material on the moth alarm clock.

7847

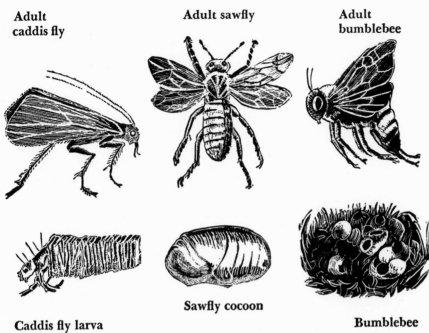

Adult caddis fly

Adult sawfly

Adult bumblebee

Caddis fly larva in case

Sawfly cocoon

Bumblebee cocoons

WHAT IS A COCOON?

Cocoons are silk houses made by some insects. These are a few of the insects that make cocoons.

Some cocoons are very small, others large. Some are tightly woven, others are loosely made. Some are tough and hard, others fragile. Sometimes leaves, hair, pebbles, bits

1

of twigs, bark, or earth are used with the silk. All are made for protection.

The cocoons that you are most likely to find are made by moths. In many parts of the United States moths are called millers. For convenience the name "moth" is used in this book. Moths have featherlike or threadlike antennae. When at rest they hold their wings level or flat against their body. Moths usually fly at night.

2

THE LIFE STORY OF MOTHS

Moths begin life as eggs. When the eggs hatch, out come caterpillars. Caterpillars are called larvae. One caterpillar is called a larva. Some people make the mistake of calling larvae "worms." Worms are not insects; they belong to another group of animals.

When the larvae first hatch out of the eggs they are very small. They soon begin to feed and grow. Before long the caterpillar's skin becomes tight and hard and he cannot grow any larger. Then the caterpillar stops eating. It is time to shed his tight skin. The skin splits open and he wiggles out. This shedding is called molting. A new skin has already been formed under the old one. The skin is soft and can stretch. In time it will become hard and tight and the caterpillar must again shed his skin if he is to continue growing.

Some caterpillars molt three times, some five times, others as many as ten times. The number of molts may vary, depending on the temperature and the amount of food the caterpillar has eaten. Each time the caterpillar molts it changes its appearance. With some there are great changes in color and markings.

3

Larva

Eggs

Newly hatched larva

Most caterpillars when fully grown make cocoons. Inside the cocoon the caterpillar changes into a dark brown mummylike pupa. *Pupa* is a word which means "doll." A scientist years ago gave it this name because he thought it looked like a doll wrapped in blankets.

4

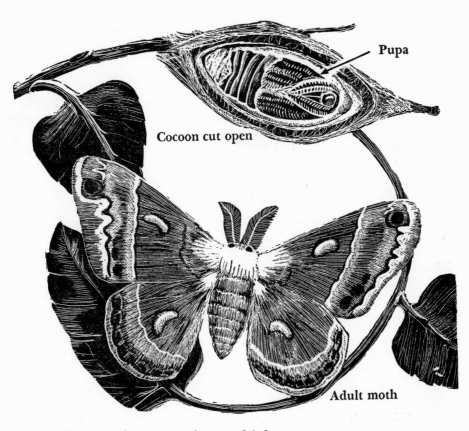

Pupa

Cocoon cut open

Adult moth

To see the pupa it would be necessary to cut open the cocoon. A close look at the pupa shows the legs, wings, and antennae of the adult moth. When the resting pupa "awakes," it sheds its skin and makes its way out of the cocoon. It is now the adult moth. Adult moths live only to lay eggs and start the life story over again.

5

HOW COCOONS ARE MADE

Making the Silk

The silk that is used in weaving the cocoon is made by the caterpillar. There are two long glands inside the caterpillar which secrete the silk. Two strands of silk pass from these glands through the storage and ducts, into a tube where they are pressed and flattened into a single silk thread. It is believed that other glands secrete a fluid which helps cement the two strands of silk together.

The flattened, ribbonlike silk thread comes out through a hollow spine on the lower lip of the caterpillar. This spine is called a spinneret. Even a newly hatched caterpillar is able to spin silk.

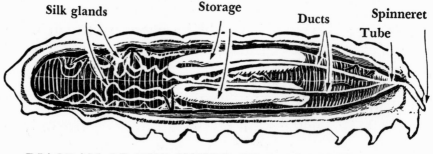

Silk glands   Storage   Ducts   Spinneret   Tube

DIAGRAM OF THE INSIDE OF A CATERPILLAR

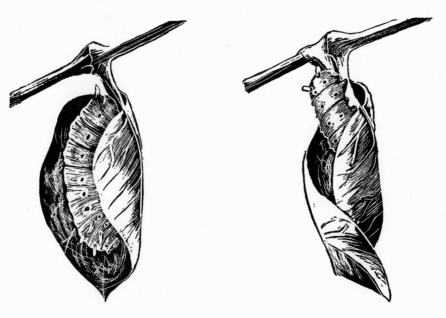

Weaving a Cocoon

Each kind of caterpillar makes its cocoon in a different way. The Promethea begins by covering the upper side of a leaf with silk. To do this it hangs upside down from the branch on which the leaf is attached. The caterpillar covers the leaf with silk as it slowly moves its head from side to side. It then covers the stem of the leaf and branch with silk threads. These threads around the stem and branch prevent the cocoon from falling to the ground in the autumn when the other leaves fall from the trees.

7

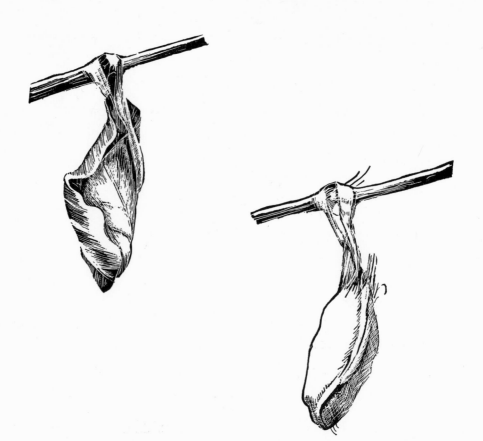

Next the caterpillar spins silk threads from one edge of the leaf to the other. As these threads dry, they shrink, and the leaf is wrapped about the caterpillar like a blanket. Inside the folded leaf the caterpillar continues to work. It is possible to hear it at work, spinning more silk and finishing its cocoon.

8

The Isabella moth (woolly bear) makes its cocoon on the ground in a sheltered spot under leaves, stones, and the like. The caterpillar spins silk threads which it wraps about itself. At the same time the caterpillar's hairs are shed. The hairs become entangled in the silk, making a dense, feltlike cocoon.

The larva of the case-making clothes moth constructs a woolen case. The case is made of tiny pieces of wool taken from the material on which the larva is feeding. They are held together with a silk lining. As the larva grows, it enlarges its case by adding more wool and silk. When time to pupate, the case becomes the cocoon.

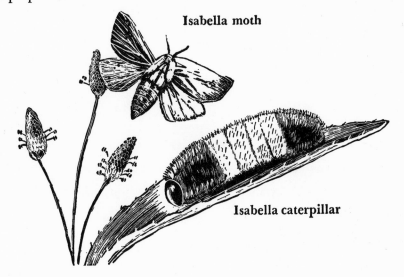

Isabella moth

Isabella caterpillar

OTHER WAYS CATERPILLARS USE SILK

Some caterpillars, like the Promethea, spin a silk carpet to cling to while shedding their skin. Others, such as the spring cankerworm, swing from trees on threads, using the threads to climb back. The caterpillars of the Io moth follow the leader. Each caterpillar spins a silk thread which the one behind follows. Some caterpillars build silk shelters which protect them while they are resting. The shelter of the tent caterpillar is one that is easy to see because of its large size. Tent caterpillars also spin paths of silk as they move about feeding. Many caterpillars spin such paths. These paths lead back to the shelter.

Spring cankerworms hanging from thread

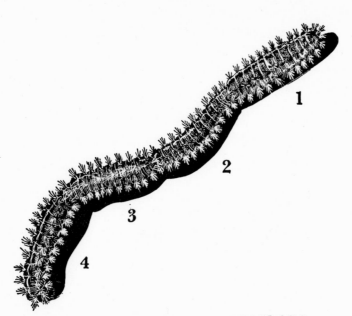

IO CATERPILLARS

THE SILK INDUSTRY

The silk that is used today in making cloth for dresses and shirts is spun by a caterpillar called the Chinese silkworm. Over four thousand years ago the Chinese discovered that the cocoon of this caterpillar could be unwound to furnish thread. A single thread three thousand feet long can be obtained from one cocoon.

COLLECTING COCOONS

Very little equipment is needed to collect cocoons. Keen eyes and persistence are the most important equipment, for cocoons are not always easy to see. A penknife, a box, a notebook, and pencil are all the rest of the equipment needed to collect cocoons.

Where to Find Them

Look on the leaves, branches, and bark of trees and shrubs. Examine fence posts, window sills, or the inside of barns and garages. Search among dead leaves and under stones on the ground. Watch for cocoons in the earth while spading the garden and digging for bait. Cocoons can be found in many places.

When to Hunt for Them

Cocoons can be found at all times of the year. It is easiest to see those that hang from the branches of trees when the trees are bare.

HOW TO COLLECT THEM

Any cocoon that is collected should be handled with care. The animal inside may be injured if the cocoon is torn, dropped, or squashed. Use a penknife to cut the twig that holds the cocoon on the tree. It will be easier to handle the cocoon if it is left attached to the twig. If possible the twig should be five to eight inches long. When removing a cocoon from bark, a fence post, or stone, do so gently. A shoe box or a similar container is useful for carrying the cocoons home.

For a collection to be valuable the following information is needed: collector's name, date collected, name of place, and where it was found. Later, when the cocoon is identified, its name should be added. A notebook can be used to keep this information.

In the search for cocoons, the homes and egg cases of other animals may be found. Many of them, for example oak apple gall, mantid egg mass, or spider egg cases, are easily mistaken for cocoons. It is fun to collect them to see what will emerge. If collected, they can be placed in a container with a fine wire top. The container should be kept out of doors in a sheltered spot.

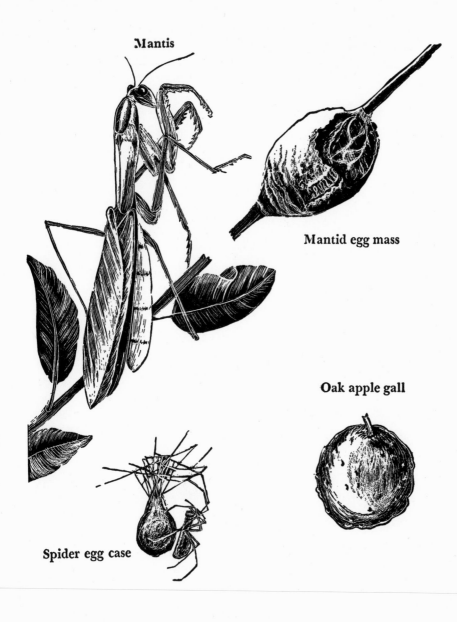

Mantis

Mantid egg mass

Oak apple gall

Spider egg case

COCOON WITH LIVE PUPA

A cocoon that has a live pupa inside is heavier than one that has a dead pupa or is empty. A person who has collected many cocoons can tell by the weight of the cocoon as it is held in his hand whether or not there is a live pupa inside. This takes practice.

When a cocoon is found, hold it firmly in the hand and shake it gently. Do not shake it hard or the animal inside may be injured. If there is a live pupa inside, it will bump against the cocoon. This dull bumping can be heard and sometimes felt. Some cocoons rattle when they are shaken. The dry pupa skin, left behind when the moth emerged, rattles inside the empty cocoon.

Some cocoons are so thinly or loosely made that it is possible to see the pupa through the cocoon.

Many cocoons that are found will be empty. The cocoon may be last year's from which the moth has already emerged. In this event it may be possible to see the opening through which it escaped.

Other cocoons may not be empty but the moth will not emerge, for the pupa is dead. Examine the cocoon carefully to see if there are any tiny holes in it. Cocoons have

16

many enemies. The ichneumon "wasp" is an insect that drills a tiny hole in a cocoon and lays her eggs inside. When the ichneumon larvae hatch, they eat the animal inside the cocoon. Instead of a moth emerging from such a cocoon, out will come many ichneumon larvae.

If an empty cocoon is found with a large ragged hole in it, it has been visited by a bird, mouse, or squirrel.

RAISING ADULTS FROM COCOONS

Only a little care is needed to raise a moth from a cocoon that has a live pupa inside. At home place the cocoon in a container. Almost any wooden box or jar will do. A clear glass jar is perhaps best for then it will be possible to see the cocoon without disturbing it. For smaller cocoons an inch or less in length, a pint or quart jar will do. For larger cocoons it is best to use at least a two-quart jar. Select a glass jar with a large opening so that once the moth has come out of the cocoon it will be possible to remove the cocoon and the moth without injuring them.

A branch should be placed in the jar so that when the moth emerges it will have something to cling to.

Fasten a piece of fine wire screening over the top of the jar. This will enable the cocoon to get air, and if the moth should come out unnoticed, it will not be able to escape. Gauze or cheesecloth can be used but they do not protect the cocoon from mice, squirrels, and other enemies.

18

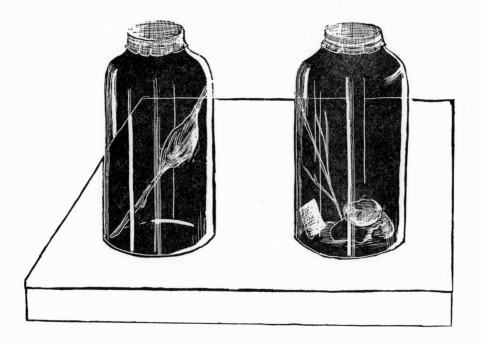

WHERE TO KEEP THE COCOON

It is best to keep the jar out of doors in a sheltered spot even in the winter. This is where the cocoon would be if it had not been collected. Out of doors the temperature and moisture are right for the cocoon. An open porch is an ideal spot. Some collectors place a cocoon between a window screen and the window. There the cocoon is in a sheltered spot out of doors and it is easy to watch.

If the cocoon is kept indoors in a warm room, water must be added to the jar or the cocoon will dry out and the animal inside will die. There is danger in adding too much water. If this is done the cocoon may become moldy. To add the proper amount of water, wet a blotter or sponge. Squeeze it to rid it of excess water. Place the blotter or sponge in the bottom of the jar. When it dries, wet it again.

A cocoon should not rest on the wet blotter or sponge. It may be necessary to build a platform in the bottom of the jar.

Do not place the jar near a radiator or in direct sunlight as it will steam. A terrarium makes an ideal place to keep cocoons indoors.

20

WHEN WILL THE MOTH EMERGE?

Many moths emerge in the spring and summer. Some emerge in the fall and winter. It is difficult to know exactly when a moth will emerge. When raising an adult from a cocoon it is helpful to know what kind of cocoon it is. Then it is possible to find out when to expect the moth to emerge. Remember that moths will emerge several weeks ahead of time when cocoons are kept indoors in a warm room.

A day or so before emerging the pupa may now and then wiggle enough to move the cocoon. With some it is possible to hear scratching sounds as the moth begins to work its way out. Some cocoons become wet at the end where the moth will emerge. With most there is no warning given.

Watching a moth emerge is very exciting. It is worth the care that has been given to the cocoon. To see this happen it will be necessary to watch the cocoon every day. It may be helpful to know that many moths usually emerge in the morning.

With some of the larger cocoons it is possible to construct a moth alarm clock. As the moth emerges, it wiggles the cocoon. This makes the ends of the wires touch and completes the circuit, causing the alarm to ring.

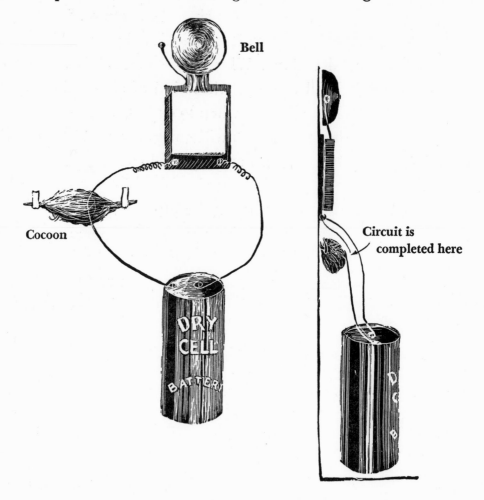

Bell

Cocoon

DRY CELL BATTERY

Circuit is completed here

When the moth first appears it is wet and crumpled. It looks as if it had been dipped in water and squeezed. Within a few hours great changes take place. Fluids pass from the body out into the wings. Gradually the wings unfold, the wings and body dry, and the moth is then ready to fly.

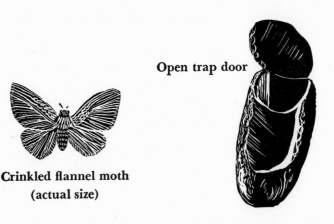

Open trap door

Crinkled flannel moth
(actual size)

HOW DO MOTHS ESCAPE FROM COCOONS?

This is one of the many questions that anyone who raises moths can help the scientist answer. It is one of many things that scientists need to know more about.

Some pupae, as in the Luna, have teeth or spines which may be used in cutting a hole in the cocoon. Polyphemus is one of many moths that secrete a liquid from the mouth which softens the silk so that the moth can push its way out. Others, such as the Promethea, appear to weave the silk thread at one end of the cocoon so that a funnellike opening is left for the moth's escape. The crinkled flannel moth escapes through a trap door built into its cocoon.

24

MATING ADULTS

When adult moths emerge, males and females of the same kind will mate and produce fertilized eggs. From these fertile eggs, caterpillars will hatch. If several cocoons have been kept and a male and female of one kind emerge at the same time, they can be placed in a cage about a foot square where they will mate.

To transfer a moth to the cage, lower a strip of cheese-cloth or gauze in front of the moth. The moth will climb onto the strip and can then be put into the cage without injury. Before transferring the moth, place branches, leaves, or strips of paper in the cage so that the female will have a place on which to lay her eggs. It is best to use a cage with wire sides rather than one with solid wood or metal sides. This will discourage the female from laying her eggs on the sides of the cage where it is difficult to remove them without injury.

There is no need to place food in the cage, as most adult moths do not feed. The few kinds that do can be released immediately after they have mated and the female has laid her eggs. Mating usually takes place within twenty-four hours after the moths emerge from the cocoons.

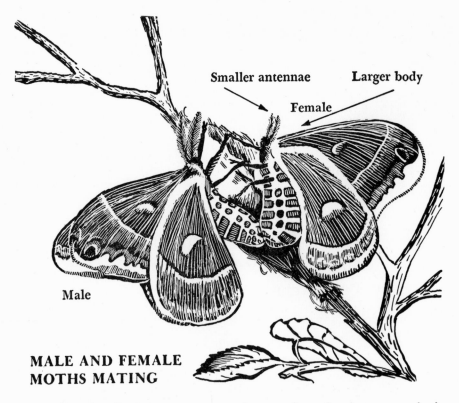

Smaller antennae   Larger body

Female

Male

**MALE AND FEMALE
MOTHS MATING**

If no males are present when a female emerges, it is possible to attract them. Put the cage out of doors with the female inside. The female gives off a strong odor which attracts males. The males that come to the cage can be caught and placed inside. After the eggs are laid, the adults can be released, or if they are wanted as specimens for a collection they can be killed.

CARE OF EGGS

Place the branches, leaves, or strips of paper with the eggs in a small container. Close the cover tightly. Store the eggs in a cool but not cold place.

If a clear glass jar or plastic box is used it will be easier to watch the color changes taking place in the eggs as they develop and to see when they hatch.

The eggs will hatch anywhere within a few days to several months, depending upon the kind of moth. The eggs of the bee moth hatch a few days after they are laid. Tent caterpillar eggs are laid in the fall and hatch the following spring.

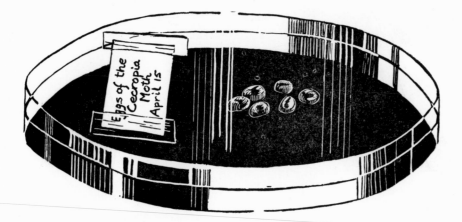

RAISING CATERPILLARS FOR COCOONS

Once the eggs have hatched it is possible to raise the caterpillars so that the actual spinning of the cocoon can be watched. Many people prefer to collect caterpillars out of doors as it is easier than mating adult moths and raising their eggs.

Not all caterpillars make cocoons. Some moth caterpillars, such as the tobacco worm, do not spin cocoons. The pupa remains naked. Others are the caterpillars of butterflies. Very few butterfly caterpillars make cocoons. Most butterfly pupae are naked. They are called chrysalids. These are the chrysalids of some butterflies.

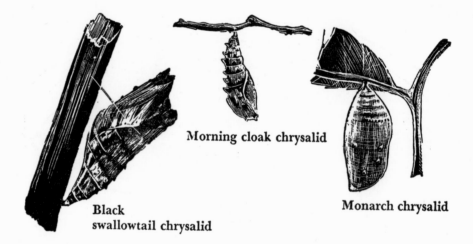

Morning cloak chrysalid

Black
swallowtail chrysalid

Monarch chrysalid

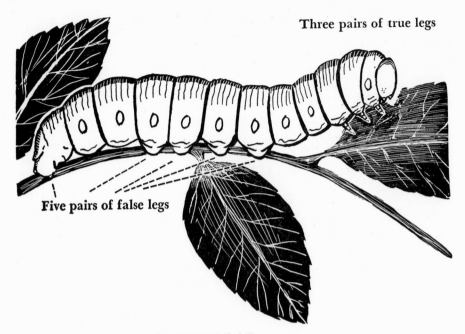

Three pairs of true legs

Five pairs of false legs

DIAGRAM OF A CATERPILLAR

It is difficult to tell whether a caterpillar is the larva of a moth or of a butterfly. Moth and butterfly caterpillars look very much alike.

The caterpillars of another group of insects—the sawflies—are sometimes mistaken for the larvae of moths and butterflies. There is a way to tell them apart. The caterpillars of sawflies have more than five pairs of false legs, unlike the caterpillar shown above.

It will be interesting to raise the caterpillars of butterflies as well as those of moths. Since the caterpillars of most butterflies change into naked pupae, without making cocoons, it is possible to watch the change take place. The caterpillar's skin becomes loose. Inside the skin the caterpillar shrinks. The wings, legs, and antennae of the adult gradually form. The animal no longer looks like a caterpillar. The pupa pushes its way out of the caterpillar skin. At first the pupa is soft. Soon its skin becomes hard and dark in color. The change from a caterpillar to a pupa may take several hours.

The best time to collect and raise caterpillars is in the summer and early fall when they are still feeding. Almost anything will serve as a cage. Here are some suggestions.

Jar of water

Screening

Lamp chimney

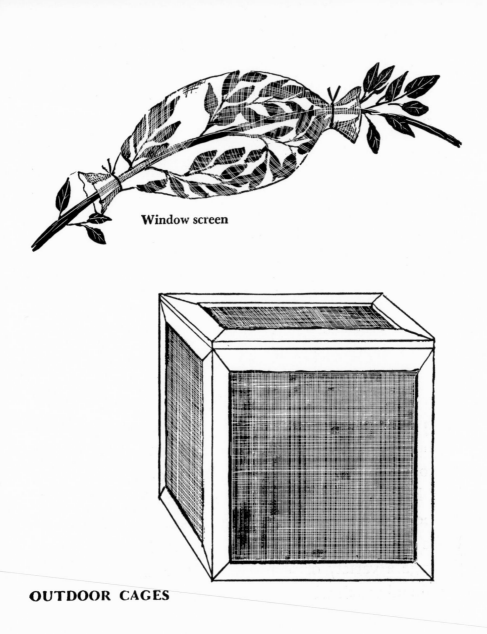

Window screen

OUTDOOR CAGES

Caterpillars can be kept indoors or out of doors. No matter where they are kept they will always need:

Food

Caterpillars are particular about the food they eat. Before caging a caterpillar observe what it is feeding on. Place the same kind of food in the cage with it. Almost all caterpillars feed on the leaves, stems, or fruits of plants. A few, such as the Peach Tree Borer, bore into wood. Some, such as the Harvester Butterfly, feed on insects. Others, like the Clothes Moth, eat wool and hair. Caterpillars eat great quantities of food. The food must be fresh. If necessary new food should be provided daily. To help keep the leaves and twigs of the food plant fresh, place them in a jar of water. The jar can be anchored in the cage with soil. Place cotton about the neck of the jar so that the caterpillars will not fall into the water and drown. Place a little soil over the cotton so that any caterpillar falling on the cotton will be able to crawl off again. If a food plant is not too big it can be potted and can be used as the bottom of the cage. If the food plant of any caterpillar is not known, place in the cage a variety of plants from the area where it was found and watch which one it chooses.

Moisture

Indoors, moisture must be added to the cage. There will be enough if a jar of water is used to hold the food plant. If a potted plant is used, the daily watering of the plant to keep it fresh will provide the needed moisture. Or place a small jar of water in the cage. The jar should be covered with gauze or cheesecloth so that the caterpillars will not fall into the water.

Air

Cover the top of the cage with fine wire screening rather than with a tight lid. If a wooden crate is being used as a cage, remove one of the sides and replace it with screening. This will allow air to circulate through the cage. Do not place the cage in direct sunlight as the inside of the cage may become too warm.

A Clean Cage

Cages must be kept clean. All waste, spoiled food, and any dead caterpillars must be removed immediately. Forceps, sticks, or a brush can be used for cleaning the cage. Keeping the cage clean will help prevent the growth of molds.

When caterpillars are about to either molt or pupate, they stop eating and act as if they were sick. The molting and the pupating periods are the most difficult in a caterpillar's life.

They should not be disturbed at this time. If it is necessary to move them to clean the cage, pick up the twig on which they are feeding or resting.

When a caterpillar is ready to spin its cocoon and pupate it will move about searching for a place to make its cocoon. Once the cocoon is made it can be kept as has already been described.

A caterpillar which is known to pupate underground should be removed from the feeding cage and placed in a glass jar that has a half inch of soil in the bottom. The soil will absorb the liquids given off as the caterpillar changes. Cover the jar with screening. The caterpillar will not be able to burrow out of sight and it will be possible to watch the caterpillar change into a pupa.

If a naked pupa is to be kept until the adult emerges, replace the screening with a tight lid and store it in a cool place. If the adult does not emerge in a few weeks, it will probably spend the winter as a pupa and emerge the following spring.

34

KEEPING A COLLECTION OF COCOONS

Once the animals have emerged, it is fun to keep a collection of cocoons. The collection can be kept in a shoe box, cigar box, or some other container. The information about each cocoon—name of moth, collector's name, date collected, name of place found, and where it was found—should be put on a label attached to each cocoon. Small and more fragile cocoons can be fastened with rubber cement, Scotch tape, or tied on an index card. The collection must be kept in a dry place or the cocoons may become

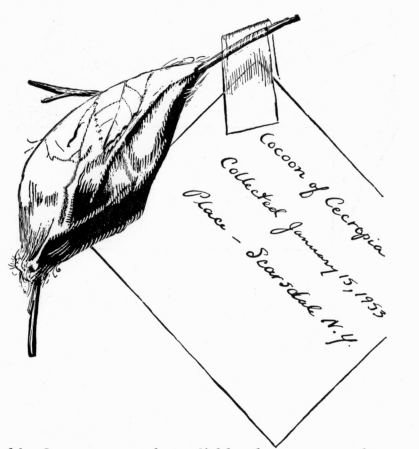

Cocoon of Cecropia
Collected January 15, 1953
Place — Scarsdale N.Y.

moldy. One teaspoon of paradichlorobenzene crystals must be placed in the container to prevent the cocoons from being damaged by insects or mold. Paradichlorobenzene crystals can be bought in most drug and hardware stores. When the crystals evaporate they should be replaced.

The following pages will help you in finding and identifying various cocoons. The common name, or nickname, of each moth is given. Alongside is the scientific, or real, name. This is the name that scientists use.

It is not necessary to know the scientific name of the different moths to enjoy collecting cocoons. But the scientific names will help in looking up other information about moths and their life stories. All illustrations are actual size unless marked "enlarged."

Polyphemus cocoon

POLYPHEMUS — [*Telea polyphemus*]

RANGE — Polyphemus is found throughout the United States.

COCOON — The cocoon is spun in the fall. It is found on the ground under trees or it may sometimes be found still hanging loosely on a tree.

In the southern states where there is a second brood, cocoons are also spun in the summer.

ADULT — The adult emerges in the spring. The adults of the second brood emerge in late summer.

CATERPILLAR — The caterpillars feed on the leaves of maple, oak, birch, apple, willow, peach, linden, and various other trees.

The large Polyphemus caterpillars are often heard before they are seen. They rear up on their false legs and make loud snapping noises with their jaws when they are disturbed.

38

POLYPHEMUS MOTH

CECROPIA — [*Platysamia cecropia*]

RANGE — Cecropia is found from the Atlantic Coast to the Rocky Mountains. Glover's silk moth, *P. gloveri,* a similar moth, is found in New Mexico, Arizona, Colorado and Wyoming. Another, the ceanothus silk moth, *P. euryalus,* is found in California, Oregon, Washington, Nevada, Utah and Wyoming.

COCOON — The cocoon is spun in the fall. It is found hanging on trees and shrubs.

ADULT — The adult emerges in the spring.

CATERPILLAR — The caterpillars feed on the leaves of apple, elm, wild cherry, spirea, and other trees and shrubs.

This cocoon is the largest and most readily found of all. The silk glands of the caterpillar can be removed and stretched to furnish gut for fish hooks and leaders used in fly fishing.

40

CECROPIA MOTH AND COCOON

CYNTHIA — [*Samia walkeri*]

RANGE — Cynthia is found in northeastern United States.

COCOON — The cocoon is spun in the fall. It is attached by silk threads, usually along the mid-rib of a compound leaf, to the twig. The attachment is several inches long.

ADULT — The adult emerges in the spring.

CATERPILLAR — The caterpillars feed mainly on ailanthus leaves, sometimes on the leaves of wild cherry, linden, sycamore, spice bush, and others.

This moth was introduced into the United States from Asia. It was hoped that the moth could be raised to furnish silk. It was found though that it is cheaper to buy silk from other countries.

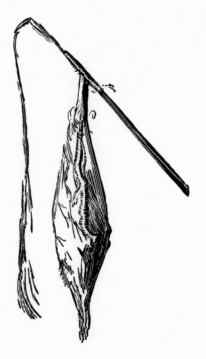

Cynthia cocoon

42

CYNTHIA MOTH

PROMETHEA — [*Callosamia promethea*]

RANGE — Promethea is found in the eastern part of the United States west to the Mississippi Valley.

COCOON — The cocoon is spun in the fall. It is like a Cynthia cocoon, but is usually attached directly to the twig and not along the midrib of a compound leaf. The attachment is usually shorter than Cynthia's.

ADULT — The adult emerges in the spring.

CATERPILLAR — The caterpillars feed on the leaves of spice bush, sassafras, wild cherry, tulip, and other trees and shrubs.

The male Promethea differs in color from the female. It is darker. Only the markings on the outer edge of the wing show. Unlike most moths which fly at night, the males of this moth fly during the day.

44

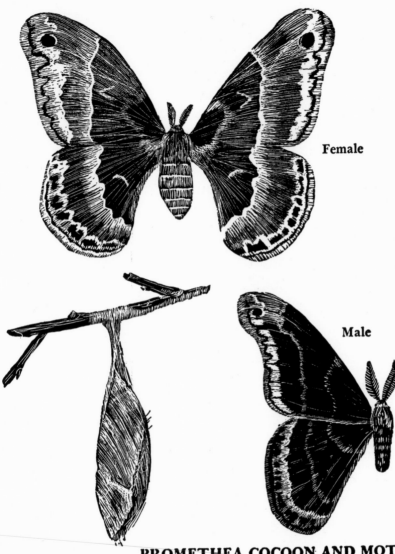

Female

Male

PROMETHEA COCOON AND MOTHS

Luna cocoon

LUNA — [*Actias luna*]

RANGE — The Luna moth is found in eastern United States west to the Great Plains.

COCOON — The cocoon is spun in the fall. It is spun among leaves on the ground in woods where nut trees grow. There may be a second brood. Then cocoons are also spun in the summer. They are easy to identify because they are thin and brittle.

ADULT — The adult emerges in the spring. The adults of the second brood emerge in the summer.

CATERPILLAR — The caterpillars feed on the leaves of walnut, hickory, birch, beech, persimmon, sweet-gum, and other trees.

The adult Luna is a favorite because of its lovely light green color and large size. The color and size, together with the long trailing edges of the hind wings, make this moth an easy one to remember. Although many people believe it to be rare, Luna is a common moth.

46

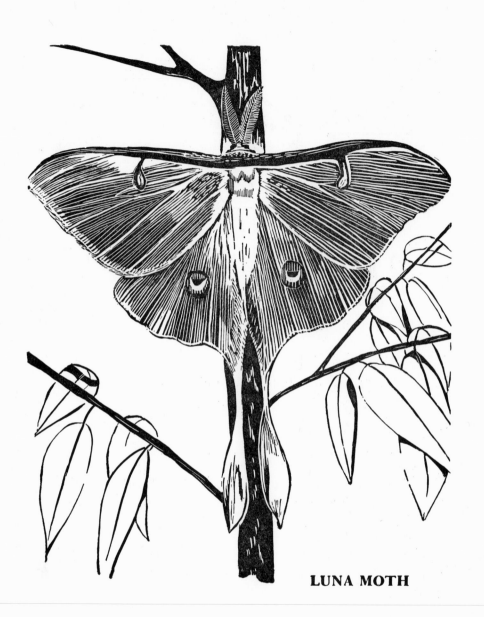

LUNA MOTH

Io moth and cocoon

IO — [*Automeris io*]

RANGE — The Io moth is found in eastern United States.

COCOON — The cocoon is spun in the fall. It is spun among leaves on the ground.

ADULT — The adult emerges in the spring.

CATERPILLAR — The caterpillars feed on the leaves of corn, cherry, apple, shadbush, oak, and other trees and shrubs.

The caterpillars of this moth should be handled carefully for they secrete an irritating fluid through their sharp spines. Use a brush to pick them up.

48

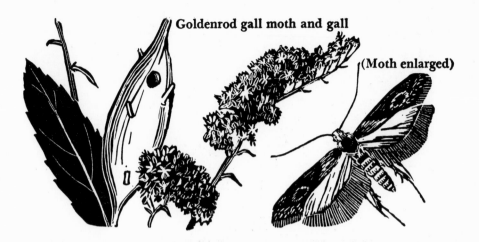

Goldenrod gall moth and gall

(Moth enlarged)

GOLDENROD GALL MOTH

[Gnorimoschema gallaesolidaginis]

RANGE — The goldenrod gall moth is found throughout the United States wherever goldenrod is found.

NO COCOON — In the spring the newly hatched caterpillar bores into the stem of a goldenrod, causing a growth to form, which is called a gall. Inside the gall in early summer the larva spins a cradle of silk and pupates.

ADULT — The adult emerges in late summer.

CATERPILLAR — The caterpillars feed on the galls.

Before pupating, the larva cuts a hole in the side of the gall and closes it with a silk plug. When the adult is ready to emerge, it pushes out the plug.

49

Isabella cocoon and moth

ISABELLA, or WOOLLY BEAR — [*Isia isabella*]

RANGE — The Isabella moth is found throughout the United States.

COCOON — The cocoon is spun in the spring and is made of the caterpillar's hairs which are fastened together with silk. It is found on the ground under stones, logs, or boards.

ADULT — The adult emerges in the spring two weeks after the cocoon is spun.

CATERPILLAR — The caterpillars feed on the leaves of grasses, plantain, dandelion, burdock, and other plants.

The caterpillars are commonly seen in the fall. They appear to be hurrying along looking for a place to spend the winter. When disturbed they curl up into a ball. This is one moth which remains in the caterpillar stage throughout the winter.

Grape leaf folder moth and cocoon

GRAPE LEAF FOLDER — [*Desmia funeralis*]

RANGE — The grape leaf folder is found in eastern United States west to the Great Plains and in California.

COCOON — The cocoon is spun in the fall. Where there are two or three broods, cocoons are also spun in the summer. The cocoons are found on grapevines or on the ground under vines.

ADULT — The adult emerges in the spring. The adults of the second and third broods emerge in the summer.

CATERPILLAR — The caterpillars feed on grape leaves, the leaves of Virginia creeper, evening primrose, and redbud.

The larvae feed on the inside of rolled leaves. The edges of the leaf are fastened together with silk threads.

51

TENT CATERPILLAR — [*Malacosoma americana*]

RANGE — This tent caterpillar is found from the Atlantic Coast west to the Rocky Mountains. Other similar tent caterpillars are found in the western states. They are *M. californica,* found in California; *M. constricta,* in Arizona, California, and Oregon; *M. fragilis,* in parts of New Mexico, Colorado, Wyoming, Montana, Utah, Nevada, California, and Oregon; and *M. pluvialis,* in Washington, Oregon, and northern California.

COCOON — The cocoon is spun in the spring. It is filled with a yellow powder. It is found in protected places on trees, fences, and buildings.

ADULT — The adult emerges in early summer.

CATERPILLAR — The caterpillars feed on the leaves of wild cherry, apple, plum, and other fruit trees.

This moth spends the winter in the egg stage. The eggs are laid in a thick band around a twig. The band is hard and has a shiny waterproof covering. The eggs hatch in early spring.

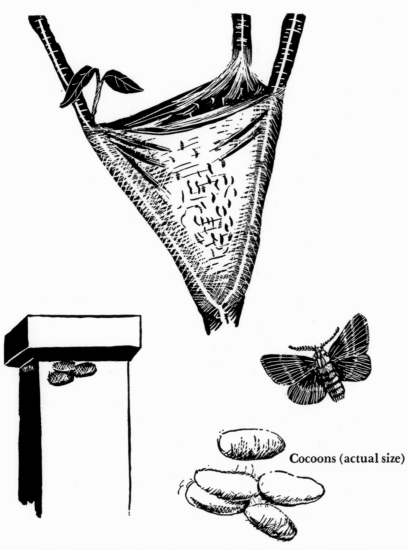

Cocoons (actual size)

TENT CATERPILLAR COCOONS AND MOTH

Bagworm cocoon

BAGWORM — [*Thyridopteryx ephemeraeformis*]

RANGE — This bagworm is found in eastern United States west to the Mississippi Valley. Other bagworm moths are found in other parts of the United States. *Oiketicus abbotii* is found in the southern states; *O. townsendi* in New Mexico and Arizona; and *O. davidsoni* in southern California.

COCOON — In the spring the newly hatched larva makes a silk bag with bits of leaves or twigs. The bag is carried about by the larva. In the fall the larva attaches the bag to a twig, lines the inside of the bag with silk, and pupates.

ADULT — The adult emerges in the fall, three weeks after the larva pupates.

54

Bagworm cocoon made on evergreen tree and moth

CATERPILLAR — The caterpillars feed on the leaves of many trees and shrubs, including evergreens.

The female does not have wings and cannot fly. She lays her eggs inside her bag, then dies. The eggs remain in the bag all winter and hatch the following spring.

CODLING MOTH, APPLE WORM
[*Carpocapsa pomonella*]

RANGE — The codling moth is found throughout the United States wherever apple or other fruit trees are grown.

COCOON — The cocoon is spun in early fall. The larva remains inside the cocoon during the winter and pupates in the spring. In the West and South where there are from two to four broods, cocoons are also spun in the summer. They are found under bark or in other protected places around fruit trees.

ADULT — The adult emerges in the spring. Where there is more than one brood, adults also emerge in the summer as well.

CATERPILLAR — The caterpillars feed on apples, pears, peaches, and other fruits. Newly hatched caterpillars feed on the leaves of the fruit trees for a short time before entering the fruit.

The eggs are laid on the outside of young fruit. Newly hatched larvae burrow in through the bottom of the growing fruit. In the South the young of the second brood are called sideworms, because they enter through the side of the fruit.

56

Cocoon

CODLING MOTH, APPLE WORM, AND COCOON

Bee in center of flower

BEE MOTH, WAX WORM — [*Galleria mellonella*]

RANGE — The bee moth is found throughout the United States wherever hives are kept.

COCOON — There are at least three broods a year. Cocoons are spun in the summer, early fall, and in the spring. They are found in and around beehives.

ADULT — Adults emerge in the spring, summer, and early fall.

CATERPILLAR — The caterpillars feed on wax made by the bees.

During the day the caterpillars remain hidden in silken tunnels inside the hives so as not to be found by the bees. At night when the bees are quiet, the caterpillars become active. They burrow through the comb, eating the wax and damaging the cells.

58

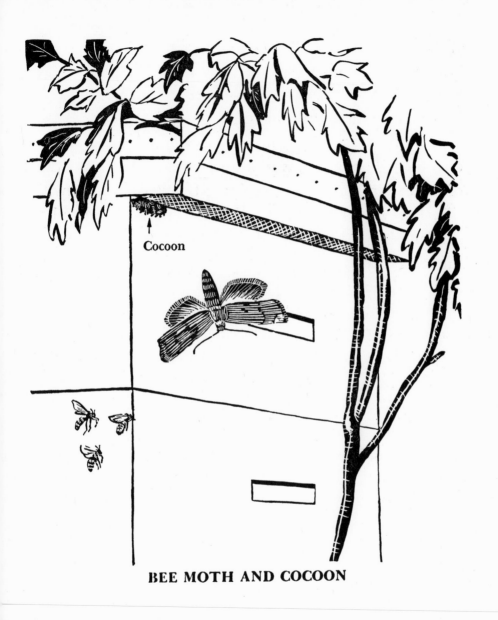

Cocoon

BEE MOTH AND COCOON

WHITE-MARKED TUSSOCK MOTH
[Hemerocampa leucostigma]

RANGE — The white-marked tussock moth is found in eastern United States west into Colorado. *H. vetusta* is a similar tussock moth found in the Pacific states.

COCOON — The cocoon is spun in early summer. It is made of the caterpillar's hairs which are fastened together with silk. It is found on tree trunks, fences, posts, and other similar places. There is a second brood. The cocoons of the second brood are spun in late summer.

ADULT — The adult emerges in midsummer. The adults of the second brood emerge in late summer and early fall.

CATERPILLAR — The caterpillars feed on the leaves of maple, elm, oak, apple, pear, and other trees.

This moth spends the winter in the egg stage. The eggs are usually laid on the cocoon of the female moth. As the female is wingless and unable to fly, she merely crawls out of her cocoon and lays her eggs on it. The eggs are protected by a frothy secretion which hardens upon drying. This moth gets its name from the four white tussocks of hair found on the larva. The California tussock moth, *H. vetusta,* feeds on young apples, causing scabs to form on the apples and spoiling them for market.

60

Cocoon

WHITE-MARKED TUSSOCK MOTH AND COCOON

EUROPEAN CORN BORER — [*Pyrausta nubilalis*]

RANGE — The European corn borer is found in the northeastern states west into Wisconsin and Indiana.

COCOON — The cocoon is spun in the spring. In Massachusetts, where there is a second brood, they are also spun in the summer. The cocoons, often only a few silk threads, are found in the stubble of corn and other plants on which the larvae feed.

ADULT — The adult emerges in the summer. The adults of the second brood emerge in late summer.

CATERPILLAR — The caterpillars feed mainly on corn plants, eating leaves, stems, and ears. In some areas they also feed on potatoes, beans, asters, dahlias, and other plants.

This moth is a serious pest. It was accidentally introduced into the United States from Europe. Great care is taken to prevent it from spreading into other parts of the country. This moth should be destroyed whenever it is found. *Do not ever try to raise the moth.*

62

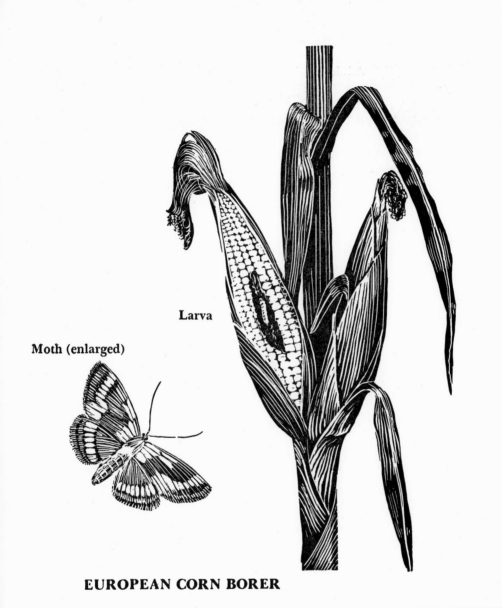

Larva

Moth (enlarged)

EUROPEAN CORN BORER

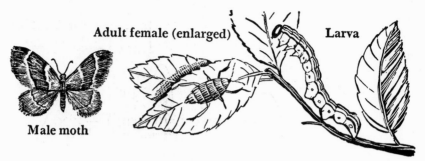

Adult female (enlarged)   Larva

Male moth

Fall cankerworm

FALL CANKERWORM — [*Alsophila pometaria*]

RANGE — The fall cankerworm is found throughout northern United States and in Colorado, New Mexico, and California.

COCOON — The cocoon is spun in early summer in cells one to four inches underground. It is usually found buried under the tree on which the larva fed.

ADULT — The adult emerges in the fall, rarely the following spring.

CATERPILLAR — The caterpillars feed on the leaves of apple, elm, and other orchard and shade trees.

The larvae are known as measuring worms, inch worms, and loopers. They were given these names because of the way in which they move. They lack prolegs in the middle of their body and must inch, or loop, along.

64

Webbing clothes moth and cocoon (enlarged)

WEBBING CLOTHES MOTH — [*Tineola biselliella*]

RANGE — The webbing clothes moth is found throughout the United States. It is more common in the East than in the West.

COCOON — Cocoons are spun throughout the year. They are found on clothing, furs, walls of closets, and in many other places.

ADULT — Adults are found throughout the year. They are most common in the summer.

CATERPILLAR — The caterpillars feed on wool, hair, fur, feathers, and other dried animal matter.

Everyone knows the damage that is done by these moths. As the larvae move about feeding they spin silken tunnels. Inside a tunnel the larva feeds for a time, then moves on to a new place and spins another tunnel. The tunnels are easier to find than the cocoons.

TOBACCO WORM or TOMATO WORM
[*Phlegethontius sexta*]

RANGE — The tobacco worm is found throughout the United States.

NO COCOON — The tobacco worm changes into a naked pupa in the fall. The pupae are found in gardens and cultivated fields in cells two to four inches underground. There is a second brood in the south. The caterpillars of the second brood pupate in the summer.

ADULT — The adult emerges in the spring. The adults of the second brood emerge in late summer.

CATERPILLAR — The caterpillars feed on the leaves of tomato, tobacco, potato, Jimson weed, and other plants.

Although most adult moths do not feed, the tobacco worm is one that does. The adult has a three-inch tongue through which it sucks the nectar of flowers. When not in use, the tongue is coiled under the head of the moth. During the pupal stage the long tongue forms the "handle" of the pupa. The caterpillars are often seen carrying small white cocoons on their back. These are the cocoons of a parasite, one of the wasps, which lays its eggs inside the caterpillar. The larvae hatch, feed on the caterpillar, and then spin the cocoons.

66

TOBACCO OR TOMATO WORM MOTH AND PUPA

YUCCA MOTH — [*Tegeticula yuccasella*]

RANGE — This yucca moth is found east of the Rocky Mountains. Other yucca moths are found in the western states. *T. maculata* is found in the Pacific states; *T. paradoxa* in the southwest. Yucca moths are found only where yucca plants grow.

COCOON — It is believed that a cocoon is spun in the fall in a cell a few inches underground around yucca plants. The moth remains in the larval stage all winter and pupates the following spring.

ADULT — The adult emerges in the spring or early summer when yuccas are in bloom.

CATERPILLAR — The caterpillars feed on the growing seeds of the yucca.

The female moth has special mouth parts for gathering pollen from a yucca plant. With the pollen she fertilizes the flower of the yucca upon which she lays her eggs. Fertilizing the flower develops seeds and provides food for the young caterpillars. Without yucca moths there would be no new yucca plants, as there is no other way in which the yuccas are fertilized. This is one example of an insect and a plant which are so dependent upon each other that neither could survive alone.

68

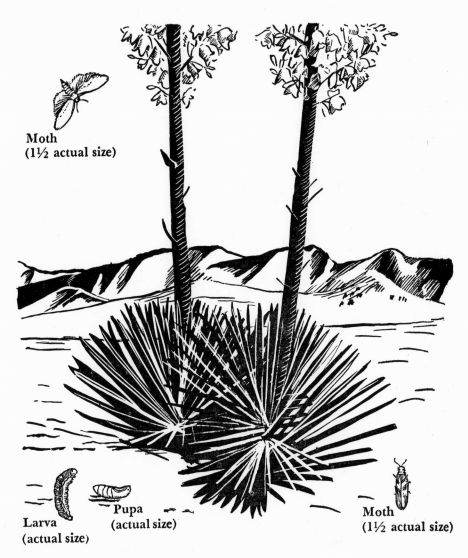

Moth
(1½ actual size)

Larva
(actual size)

Pupa
(actual size)

Moth
(1½ actual size)

YUCCA MOTH

WHERE TO GO FOR OTHER INFORMATION

Your school or public library will probably have the following books:

Caterpillars and Their Moths, by I. M. Eliot and C. M. Soule, The Century Company, New York, 1902. Out of print.

This book has detailed life stories of many moths.

The Tale of the Promethea Moth, by Henry B. Kane, Alfred A. Knopf, New York, 1942. Wild World Series, Vol. 3.

Excellent photographs and drawings showing the life of the moth.

The Moth Book, by W. J. Holland, Doubleday, Page and Company, Garden City, New York, 1922. Out of print.

This book has illustrations of adult moths which will help in their identification.

The Insect Guide, by Ralph Swain, Doubleday and Company, New York, 1948.

A good general reference book on insects, well illustrated.

Field Book of Insects, by Frank E. Lutz, G. P. Putnam's Sons, New York, 1935, revised edition, 1948.

A good general reference book on insects.

The Boys' Book of Insects, by Edwin Way Teale, E. P. Dutton and Company, Inc., New York, 1939.

A general book on insects. Good suggestions for insect study.

A visit to a museum of natural history where collections are on display will be helpful in answering many questions the collector may have.

INDEX